In memory of

PHIL SHELDON (1953-2005)

and

RICHARD WHITELEY (1943-2005)

Two friends who loved cricket
and missed a wonderful summer.

First published in 2005 by

A & C Black Ltd, 38 Soho Square, London W1D 3HB
www.acblack.com
and
John Wisden & Co Ltd, 13 Old Aylesfield, Golden Pot, Alton, Hampshire GU34 4BY
www.wisden.com www.cricinfo.com

A copy of the CIP entry for this book is available from the British Library.

ISBN-10: 0-7136-7745-7
ISBN-13: 9-780-7136-7745-4

10 9 8 7 6 5 4 3 2 1

A & C Black uses paper produced with elemental chlorine-free pulp,
harvested from managed sustainable forests.

Design by five-twentyfive
Text by Lawrence Booth
Project management by Nicky Thompson
Printed and bound in Dubai by Oriental Press

THE ASHES IN FOCUS

PATRICK EAGAR

A & C Black • London   John Wisden & Co Ltd

CONTENTS

FOREWORD

One of the great joys of cricket is the wide diversity of those who take part in the game on the field, as well as the people who tell the story of a day's play to millions of cricket lovers around the world.

Patrick Eagar made his Test-match debut as a photographer in the first Test of a gripping series in 1972 when Ian Chappell's Australians toured England, and in his opening encounter at international level he recorded Ray Illingworth leading England to another victory.

Some brilliant photographs of that Old Trafford encounter were satisfying enough, but then he had "Massie's Match" at Lord's with the Australian debutant taking 16 wickets for 137 in his first game and Greg Chappell hitting one of the more majestic centuries seen at Test-match level.

There's not much even the finest photographer can do to enrapture his audience with a close-up of *Fusarium Oxysporum*, the extraordinary grass fungus which had attacked the Headingley fourth-Test pitch with great vigour. Patrick did his best with Derek Underwood's splendid 10 wickets in the match.

The Oval, with Ian and Greg Chappell providing the first instance of brothers scoring Test hundreds in the same innings, produced a fitting end to the series. I doubt that Patrick could have asked for more and, in its own way, it was a similar series to the 2005 Ashes battle with so much depending on the final match, where I was also working, this time for Channel 4 Television.

It was good to watch him in action because of the Hampshire connection between us. I had played for Australia against the county in 1953 when his father, Desmond, was captain. Then I captained Australia in 1961 at the Southampton ground when Colin Ingleby-Mackenzie led them and Colin and I broached a bottle of champagne in anticipation of Hampshire winning the Championship for the first time.

This summer, Patrick and I were two of many people charged with the delightful job of recording the action in one of the greatest Ashes battles in the history of the game, and Patrick has it all in the pages of this book. No one knows better the patience required to finish up with a high-class photograph; no one is better at judging to the fraction of a second the moment that changes a good photograph into a great one.

Richie Benaud

INTRODUCTION

The history of sport is littered with misplaced hyperbole, but in the case of the 2005 Ashes it occasionally felt as if even hyperbole was not enough. To conjure up one thriller in a five-Test series might be regarded as good fortune. To have three, plus a finale at The Oval that was not far behind, was simply outrageous. By the time England had completed a 2-1 victory to regain the Ashes for the first time since 1986-87, the country that had given birth to the game was hailing it like a prodigal son. The tabloids proudly proclaimed that cricket was coming home. The truth, perhaps, was that it had never really been away.

Yet when Australia won the first Test at Lord's at a canter, few could have predicted the tension that would follow. As one Test gave way to another, it was as if each was trying to outdo the last. At Edgbaston, England won by two runs. At Old Trafford, they came within a single wicket of victory. And at Trent Bridge, they squeezed home by the skin of their teeth, despite having asked Australia to follow on. Even at The Oval, it needed a breathtaking century from Kevin Pietersen to steer England to safety with the series in the balance at lunch on the final day.

Their hero, though, was Andrew Flintoff, who scored 402 runs, took 24 wickets, and did it all with the kind of modesty which a football-mad nation had long forgotten. He was rewarded with the freedom of his home town of Preston, and a large slice of Ashes immortality.

With a little more luck, the same might have been said of Shane Warne. He carried Australia's attack almost single-handedly to take 40 wickets and proved more than handy with the bat. Nothing was more cruelly ironic than the catch he missed off Pietersen on the final day of the series. At the same time, it was strangely fitting - one last twist in a summer full of them.

ever had a Test match experienced a build-up like it. They were writing about Lord's roughly a year before it happened, and in one or two cases even earlier. Australia, the world champions, had been whitewashing opponents at will. England, ranked No. 2, had beaten West Indies twice, as well as New Zealand and South Africa. The stage was set, and few stages are set more elegantly than the home of cricket. In the days leading up to the game interest peaked to almost impossible levels. Michael Vaughan was only half-joking when he said both sides were "sick and tired of talking about the Ashes". Glenn McGrath went ahead regardless and predicted a 5-0 win for Australia. But the time for kidology had stopped. The greatest series of them all was about to begin.

FIRST TEST

LORD'S 21 – 24 JULY 2005

Australia won by 239 runs

above Nervous tension in the St John's Wood air.

left Two British traditions: the first morning of the Lord's Test against Australia. And a queue.

right Ricky Ponting calls correctly and Australia will bat first.

previous pages Kevin Pietersen's six off Glenn McGrath was one of the few English moments which had the members on their feet.

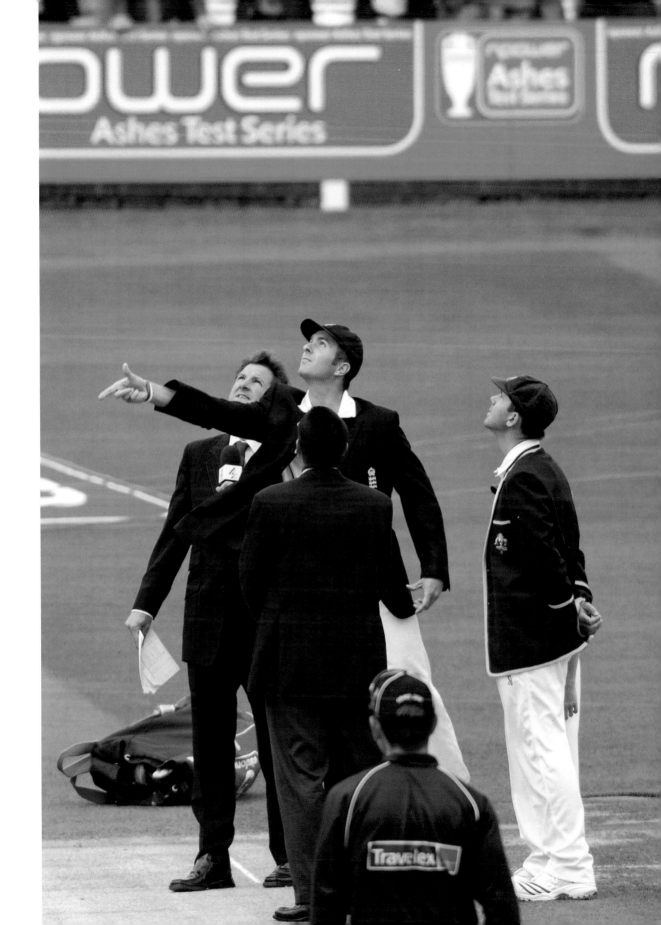

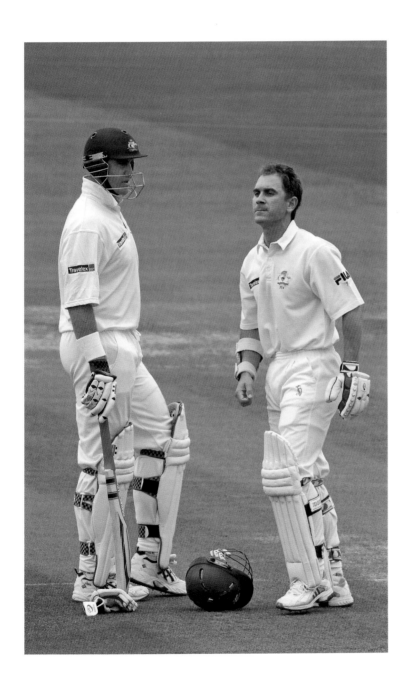

opposite *Steve Harmison hits Justin Langer with the second ball of the series and, at long last, Australia know they have a game on their hands.*

THURSDAY 10:31 AM

left *Matthew Hayden looks concerned; Langer just looks uncomfortable.*

THURSDAY 10:32 AM

above **First blood to England as Matthew Hoggard sneaks one through Matthew Hayden's defences.**

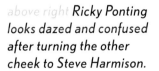

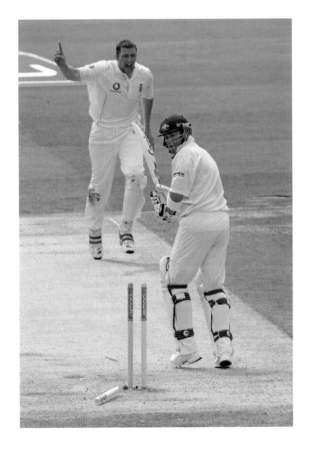

above right **Ricky Ponting**
looks dazed and confused
after turning the other
cheek to Steve Harmison.

right **The Australian**
collapse continues as
Harmison knocks back
Shane Warne's leg stump.

top Glenn McGrath
persuades Marcus
Trescothick to edge
to third slip ...
THURSDAY 3.33

above ... and Australia
have their first wicket.
THURSDAY 3.33

right For McGrath,
though, it is No. 500.
Among fast bowlers,
only Courtney Walsh
of West Indies, with 519,
now lay in wait.
THURSDAY 3.34

above **Machines do not get much more well oiled than Glenn McGrath. His spell of five for two in 31 balls on the first day at Lord's was smoothness itself.**

THURSDAY 5.02 PM

left **McGrath castles Michael Vaughan and England are 18 for three.**

below **Brett Lee goes aerial after bouncing out Geraint Jones. It's now 79 for six.**

top **Geraint Jones drops Jason Gillespie off Simon Jones, and English heads go in the same direction.**

above **Andrew Flintoff joins in by spilling Glenn McGrath ...**

right **... and Jones cannot quite believe his luck.**

opposite **Jones shows his team-mates how to do it by clinging on to Simon Katich's cut on the third-man fence.**

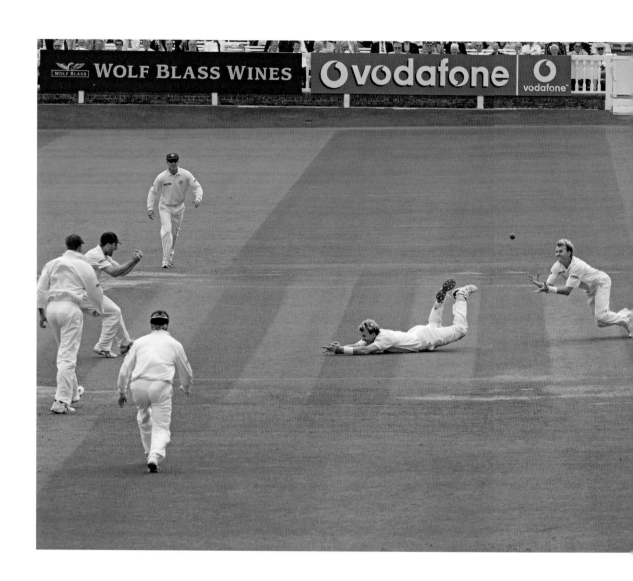

above **Andrew Strauss
watches as if in slow
motion as Brett Lee
clings on athletically to a
return chance. England's
slide is under way.**

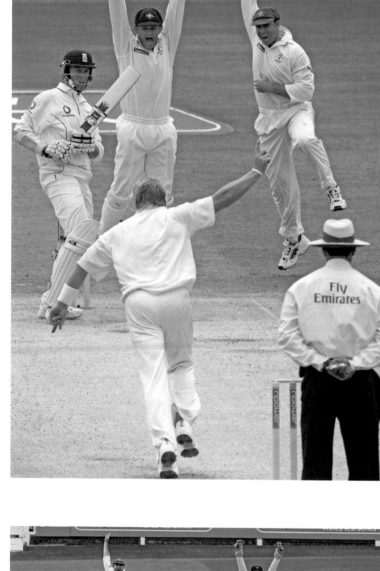

left Matthew Hayden catches Marcus Trescothick at slip off Shane Warne and England begin to look like a beaten side.
SATURDAY

below Ian Bell pads up to Warne with fatal consequences. Aleem Dar prepares to raise his finger.
SATURDAY

top **Michael Vaughan's
off stump goes missing
once more, this time
courtesy of Brett Lee.**

centre **Andrew Flintoff
looks away guiltily
after edging a cut off
Shane Warne.**

right **England's
procession continues as
Glenn McGrath traps
Matthew Hoggard.**

above Simon Jones
edges Glenn McGrath
to Shane Warne ...

left ... and Australia
have won by 239 runs.

FIRST TEST

LORD'S

Toss: Australia
Umpires: Aleem Dar (Pak) and RE Koertzen (SA)
Man of the Match: GD McGrath
AUSTRALIA WON BY 239 RUNS

AUSTRALIA 1ST INNINGS

		R	M	B	4	6
JL Langer	c Harmison b Flintoff	40	77	44	5	0
ML Hayden	b Hoggard	12	38	25	2	0
RT Ponting*	c Strauss b Harmison	9	38	18	1	0
DR Martyn	c GO Jones b SP Jones	2	13	4	0	0
MJ Clarke	lbw b SP Jones	11	35	22	2	0
SM Katich	c GO Jones b Harmison	27	107	67	5	0
AC Gilchrist †	c GO Jones b Flintoff	26	30	19	6	0
SK Warne	b Harmison	28	40	29	5	0
B Lee	c GO Jones b Harmison	3	13	8	0	0
JN Gillespie	lbw b Harmison	1	19	11	0	0
GD McGrath	not out	10	9	6	2	0
Extras	(b 5, lb 4, w 1, nb 11)	21				
Total	(40.2 overs, 209 mins)	**190**				

FoW: 1-35 (Hayden, 7.6 ov) 2-55 (Ponting, 12.5 ov) 3-66 (Langer, 14.4 ov) 4-66 (Martyn, 15.1 ov) 5-87 (Clarke, 21.5 ov) 6-126 (Gilchrist, 28.3 ov) 7-175 (Warne, 36.1 ov) 8-178 (Katich, 36.3 ov) 9-178 (Lee, 38.4 ov) 10-190 (Gillespie, 40.2 ov)

BOWLING	O	M	R	W	
Harmison	11.2	0	43	5	
Hoggard	8	0	40	1	(2nb)
Flintoff	11	2	50	2	(9nb)
SP Jones	10	0	48	2	(1w)

AUSTRALIA 2ND INNINGS

		R	M	B	4	6
JL Langer	run out (Pietersen)	6	24	15	1	0
ML Hayden	b Flintoff	34	65	54	5	0
RT Ponting*	c sub (JC Hildreth) b Hoggard	42	100	65	3	0
DR Martyn	lbw b Harmison	65	215	138	8	0
MJ Clarke	b Hoggard	91	151	106	15	0
SM Katich	c SP Jones b Harmison	67	177	113	8	0
AC Gilchrist †	b Flintoff	10	26	14	1	0
SK Warne	c Giles b Harmison	2	13	7	0	0
B Lee	run out (Giles)	8	16	16	1	0
JN Gillespie	b SP Jones	13	72	52	3	0
GD McGrath	not out	20	44	32	3	0
Extras	(b 10, lb 8, nb 8)	26				
Total	(100.4 overs, 457 mins)	**384**				

FoW: 1-18 (Langer, 5.3 ov) 2-54 (Hayden, 14.4 ov) 3-100 (Ponting, 27.3 ov) 4-255 (Clarke, 61.6 ov) 5-255 (Martyn, 62.1 ov) 6-274 (Gilchrist, 67.2 ov) 7-279 (Warne, 70.2 ov) 8-289 (Lee, 74.1 ov) 9-341 (Gillespie, 89.6 ov) 10-384 (Katich, 100.4 ov)

BOWLING	O	M	R	W	
Harmison	27.4	6	54	3	
Hoggard	16	1	56	2	(2nb)
Flintoff	27	4	123	2	(5nb)
SP Jones	18	1	69	1	(1nb)
Giles	11	1	56	0	
Bell	1	0	8	0	

ENGLAND 1ST INNINGS

		R	M	B	4	6
ME Trescothick	c Langer b McGrath	4	24	17	1	0
AJ Strauss	c Warne b McGrath	2	28	21	0	0
MP Vaughan*	b McGrath	3	29	20	0	0
IR Bell	b McGrath	6	34	25	1	0
KP Pietersen	c Martyn b Warne	57	148	89	8	2
A Flintoff	b McGrath	0	8	4	0	0
GO Jones †	c Gilchrist b Lee	30	85	56	6	0
AF Giles	c Gilchrist b Lee	11	14	13	2	0
MJ Hoggard	c Hayden b Warne	0	18	16	0	0
SJ Harmison	c Martyn b Lee	11	35	19	1	0
SP Jones	not out	20	21	14	3	0
Extras	(b 1, lb 5, nb 5)	11				
Total	(48.1 overs, 227 mins)	**155**				

FoW: 1-10 (Trescothick, 6.1 ov) 2-11 (Strauss, 6.5 ov) 3-18 (Vaughan, 12.2 ov) 4-19 (Bell, 14.3 ov) 5-21 (Flintoff, 16.1 ov) 6-79 (GO Jones, 34.1 ov) 7-92 (Giles, 36.6 ov) 8-101 (Hoggard, 41.4 ov) 9-122 (Pietersen, 43.4 ov) 10-155 (Harmison, 48.1 ov)

BOWLING	O	M	R	W	
McGrath	18	5	53	5	
Lee	15.1	5	47	3	(4nb)
Gillespie	8	1	30	0	(1nb)
Warne	7	2	19	2	

ENGLAND 2ND INNINGS (TARGET: 420)

		R	M	B	4	6
ME Trescothick	c Hayden b Warne	44	128	103	8	0
AJ Strauss	c & b Lee	37	115	67	6	0
MP Vaughan*	b Lee	4	47	26	1	0
IR Bell	lbw b Warne	8	18	15	0	0
KP Pietersen	not out	64	120	79	6	2
A Flintoff	c Gilchrist b Warne	3	14	11	0	0
GO Jones †	c Gillespie b McGrath	6	51	27	1	0
AF Giles	c Hayden b McGrath	0	2	2	0	0
MJ Hoggard	lbw b McGrath	0	18	15	0	0
SJ Harmison	lbw b Warne	0	3	1	0	0
SP Jones	c Warne b McGrath	0	12	6	0	0
Extras	(b 6, lb 5, nb 3)	14				
Total	(58.1 overs, 268 mins)	**180**				

FoW: 1-80 (Strauss, 26.3 ov) 2-96 (Trescothick, 29.2 ov) 3-104 (Bell, 33.1 ov) 4-112 (Vaughan, 36.2 ov) 5-119 (Flintoff, 39.3 ov) 6-158 (GO Jones, 50.3 ov) 7-158 (Giles, 50.5 ov) 8-164 (Hoggard, 54.6 ov) 9-167 (Harmison, 55.3 ov) 10-180 (SP Jones, 58.1 ov)

BOWLING	O	M	R	W	
McGrath	17.1	2	29	4	
Lee	15	3	58	2	(1nb)
Gillespie	6	0	18	0	(2nb)
Warne	20	2	64	4	

The fear after the first Test was that England would be blown away like the local rooftops during the tornado which had skirted round Edgbaston the previous week. But while Australia were treating Lord's like the start of another Ashes procession, England were determined to regard it as an aberration and named an unchanged side. The drama began while the ground was still filling up.

With 45 minutes to go before the toss, Glenn McGrath trod on a cricket ball on the outfield, twisted his right ankle and was driven off the pitch in agony. Ricky Ponting then added misjudgment to misfortune by inviting England to bat, a decision which Michael Vaughan would later identify as the series turning-point. But first there was a game to be won. And it was a game that would go down in folklore.

SECOND TEST

EDGBASTON 4 – 7 AUGUST 2005

England won by two runs

above **Shane Warne drops Andrew Strauss on four off Jason Gillespie. England's openers go on to add 112.**
THURSDAY 10.44 AM

right **Marcus Trescothick's 90 kickstarted England's first-day rush to 407. Australia are open-mouthed.**
THURSDAY 12.12 PM

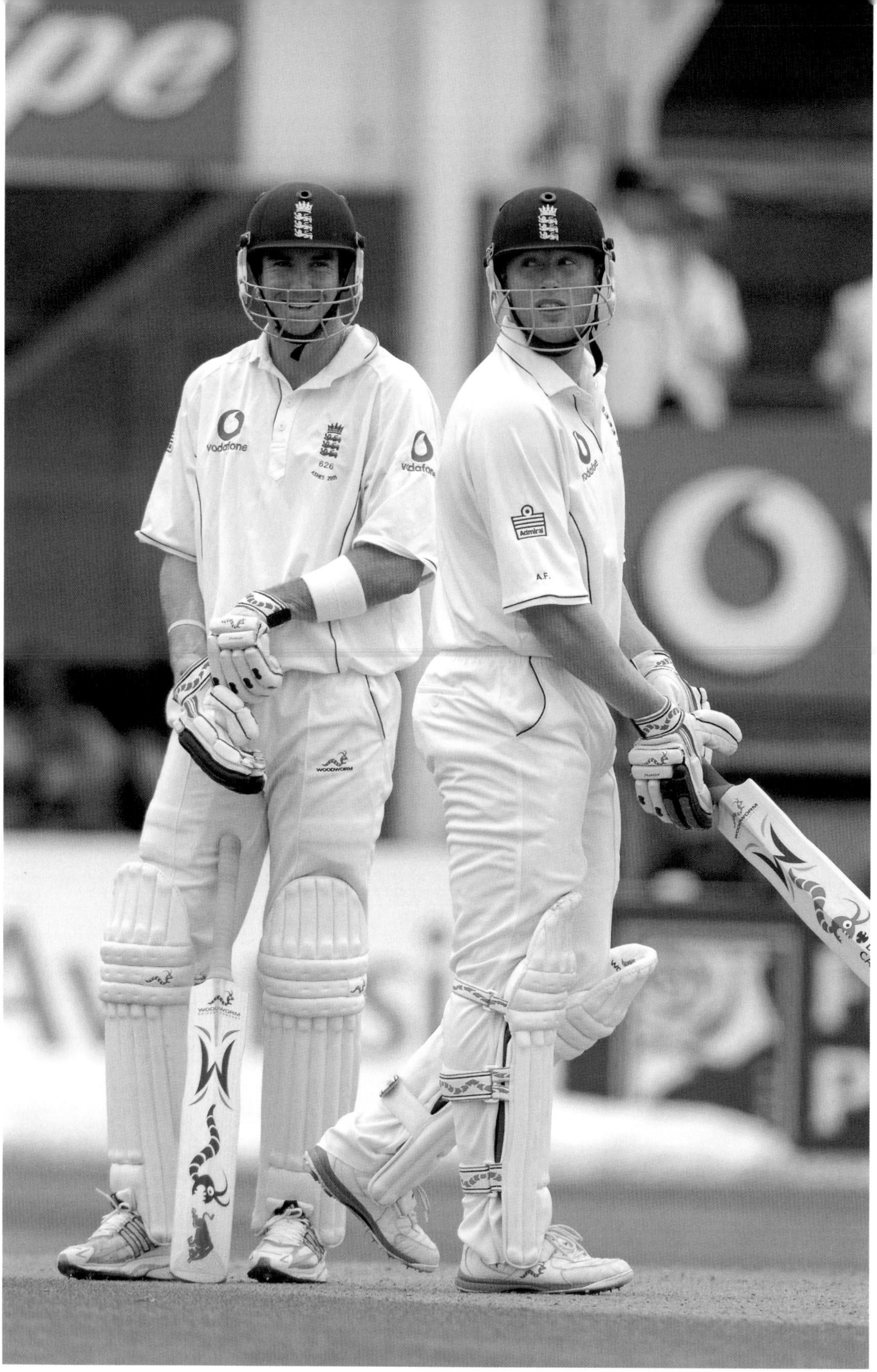
vodafone
626
Admiral
WOODWORM
A.F.

right **Andrew Flintoff mows Shane Warne for six.**

left **England's great white hopes, Kevin Pietersen and Flintoff, added 103 for the fifth wicket.**

below **Not everyone enjoyed Pietersen's bottom-handed technique, but at times it was devastating.**

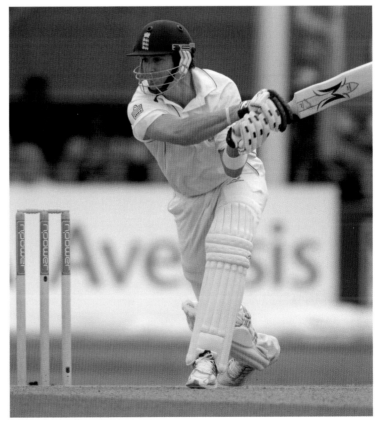

left *Ashley Giles ignored the critics to take three crucial wickets in Australia's first innings.*
FRIDAY 2:17 PM

right *Giles celebrates the demise of Michael Clarke.*
FRIDAY 2:32 PM

below *Shane Warne is bowled on the charge for eight.*
FRIDAY 4:24 PM

above *Andrew Strauss is bamboozled by a huge Shane Warne leg break, and England face a sleepless night.*

above **Brett Lee bowls Michael Vaughan and England are 29 for three.**

left **Geraint Jones is given a life thanks to Jason Gillespie's juggling.**

right **With all nine fielders on the fence, Andrew Flintoff still launches Lee out of the ground ...**

left **Billy Bowden confirms
what everyone knew
anyway – Andrew Flintoff
has just hit another six.**

above **The fun ends as
Flintoff fails to connect
with a heave against
Shane Warne. Australia
need 282 to win.**

above **Ricky Ponting is out for a duck and Australia are 48 for two.**

left **Trescothick again, this time after Matthew Hayden edges Simon Jones.**

above **Simon Katich
looks back to see Marcus
Trescothick hold on at
slip – but only just.**
SATURDAY 12.58 PM

right **Andrew Flintoff
inflicts another nought, this
time on Jason Gillespie.**
SATURDAY 3.52 PM

above **The last ball of the day and Steve Harmison confounds Michael Clarke with an inch-perfect slow yorker.**
SATURDAY 6.11PM

right **Warne uppercuts Harmison for four and Australia are beginning to believe.**

above Shane Warne is in a
tangle after treading on his
stumps. England need one
more wicket, Australia 62 runs.

opposite, top Brett Lee takes one
on the body from Andrew Flintoff.

right Flintoff throws everything at
Lee as England grow increasingly
desperate.

opposite, bottom Steve Harmison
digs one in, Michael Kasprowicz
flinches ... and Geraint Jones
stoops to seal a last-ditch win.

previous pages England are beside themselves as Billy Bowden raises his crooked finger. Michael Kasprowicz and Brett Lee don't know where to look.

above Steve Harmison is swamped and the Ashes are alive.

SECOND TEST

EDGBASTON

Toss: Australia
Umpires: BF Bowden (NZ) and RE Koertzen (SA)
Man of the Match: A Flintoff
ENGLAND WON BY TWO RUNS

ENGLAND 1ST INNINGS

		R	M	B	4	6
ME Trescothick	c Gilchrist b Kasprowicz	90	143	102	15	2
AJ Strauss	b Warne	48	113	76	10	0
MP Vaughan*	c Lee b Gillespie	24	54	41	3	0
IR Bell	c Gilchrist b Kasprowicz	6	2	3	1	0
KP Pietersen	c Katich b Lee	71	152	76	10	1
A Flintoff	c Gilchrist b Gillespie	68	74	62	6	5
GO Jones †	c Gilchrist b Kasprowicz	1	14	15	0	0
AF Giles	lbw b Warne	23	34	30	4	0
MJ Hoggard	lbw b Warne	16	62	49	2	0
SJ Harmison	b Warne	17	16	11	2	1
SP Jones	not out	19	39	24	1	1
Extras	(lb 9, w 1, nb 14)	24				
Total	(79.2 overs, 356 mins)	407				

FoW: 1-112 (Strauss, 25.3 ov) 2-164 (Trescothick, 32.3 ov) 3-170 (Bell, 32.6 ov) 4-187 (Vaughan, 36.6 ov) 5-290 (Flintoff, 54.3 ov) 6-293 (GO Jones, 57.4 ov) 7-342 (Giles, 65.1 ov) 8-348 (Pietersen, 66.3 ov) 9-375 (Harmison, 69.4 ov) 10-407 (Hoggard, 79.2 ov)

BOWLING

	O	M	R	W	
Lee	17	1	111	1	(3nb, 1w)
Gillespie	22	3	91	2	(3nb)
Kasprowicz	15	3	80	3	(8nb)
Warne	25.2	4	116	4	

ENGLAND 2ND INNINGS

		R	M	B	4	6
ME Trescothick	c Gilchrist b Lee	21	51	38	4	0
AJ Strauss	b Warne	6	28	12	1	0
MJ Hoggard	c Hayden b Lee	1	35	27	0	0
MP Vaughan*	b Lee	1	2	2	0	0
IR Bell	c Gilchrist b Warne	21	69	43	2	0
KP Pietersen	c Gilchrist b Warne	20	50	35	0	2
A Flintoff	b Warne	73	133	86	6	4
GO Jones †	c Ponting b Lee	9	33	19	1	0
AF Giles	c Hayden b Warne	8	44	36	0	0
SJ Harmison	c Ponting b Warne	0	2	1	0	0
SP Jones	not out	12	42	23	3	0
Extras	(lb 1, nb 9)	10				
Total	(52.1 overs, 249 mins)	182				

FoW: 1-25 (Strauss, 6.2 ov) 2-27 (Trescothick, 11.2 ov) 3-29 (Vaughan, 11.5 ov) 4-31 (Hoggard, 13.5 ov) 5-72 (Pietersen, 24.6 ov) 6-75 (Bell, 26.5 ov) 7-101 (GO Jones, 33.6 ov) 8-131 (Giles, 44.3 ov) 9-131 (Harmison, 44.4 ov) 10-182 (Flintoff, 52.1 ov)

BOWLING

	O	M	R	W	
Lee	18	1	82	4	(5nb)
Gillespie	8	0	24	0	(1nb)
Kasprowicz	3	0	29	0	(3nb)
Warne	23.1	7	46	6	

AUSTRALIA 1ST INNINGS

		R	M	B	4	6
JL Langer	lbw b SP Jones	82	276	154	7	0
ML Hayden	c Strauss b Hoggard	0	5	1	0	0
RT Ponting*	c Vaughan b Giles	61	87	76	12	0
DR Martyn	run out (Vaughan)	20	23	18	4	0
MJ Clarke	c GO Jones b Giles	40	85	68	7	0
SM Katich	c GO Jones b Flintoff	4	22	18	1	0
AC Gilchrist †	not out	49	120	69	4	0
SK Warne	b Giles	8	14	14	2	0
B Lee	c Flintoff b SP Jones	6	14	10	1	0
JN Gillespie	lbw b Flintoff	7	36	37	1	0
MS Kasprowicz	lbw b Flintoff	0	1	1	0	0
Extras	(b 13, lb 7, w 1, nb 10)	31				
Total	(76 overs, 346 mins)	308				

FoW: 1-0 (Hayden, 1.1 ov) 2-88 (Ponting, 19.5 ov) 3-118 (Martyn, 24.5 ov) 4-194 (Clarke, 44.2 ov) 5-208 (Katich, 49.4 ov) 6-262 (Langer, 61.3 ov) 7-273 (Warne, 64.5 ov) 8-282 (Lee, 67.1 ov) 9-308 (Gillespie, 75.5 ov) 10-308 (Kasprowicz, 75.6 ov)

BOWLING

	O	M	R	W	
Harmison	11	1	48	0	(2nb)
Hoggard	8	0	41	1	(4nb)
SP Jones	16	2	69	2	(1nb, 1w)
Flintoff	15	1	52	3	(3nb)
Giles	26	2	78	3	

AUSTRALIA 2ND INNINGS (TARGET: 282)

		R	M	B	4	6
JL Langer	b Flintoff	28	54	47	4	0
ML Hayden	c Trescothick b SP Jones	31	106	64	4	0
RT Ponting*	c GO Jones b Flintoff	0	4	5	0	0
DR Martyn	c Bell b Hoggard	28	64	36	5	0
MJ Clarke	b Harmison	30	101	57	4	0
SM Katich	c Trescothick b Giles	16	27	21	3	0
AC Gilchrist †	c Flintoff b Giles	1	8	4	0	0
JN Gillespie	lbw b Flintoff	0	4	2	0	0
SK Warne	hit wicket b Flintoff	42	79	59	4	2
B Lee	not out	43	99	75	5	0
MS Kasprowicz	c GO Jones b Harmison	20	60	31	3	0
Extras	(b 13, lb 8, w 1, nb 18)	40				
Total	(64.3 overs, 307 mins)	279				

FoW: 1-47 (Langer, 12.2 ov) 2-48 (Ponting, 12.6 ov) 3-82 (Hayden, 22.5 ov) 4-107 (Martyn, 26.1 ov) 5-134 (Katich, 31.6 ov) 6-136 (Gilchrist, 33.5 ov) 7-137 (Gillespie, 34.2 ov) 8-175 (Clarke, 43.4 ov) 9-220 (Warne, 52.1 ov) 10-279 (Kasprowicz, 64.3 ov)

BOWLING

	O	M	R	W	
Harmison	17.3	3	62	2	(1nb, 1w)
Hoggard	5	0	26	1	
Giles	15	3	68	2	
Flintoff	22	3	79	4	(13nb)
SP Jones	5	1	23	1	

The Edgbaston epic had put pressure on the rest of the series by setting new standards of excitement. But with only three days' rest between that game and this one, the players could hardly be expected to scale the heights again. Or could they? Australia were now fully aware that they were in a battle, and their decision to rush Glenn McGrath back into the side, when he had barely recovered from his ankle injury, came with a faint whiff of panic. Michael Kasprowicz missed out, while England, still riding the crest of their Birmingham wave, stuck with the same side. And when Michael Vaughan finally won a toss, a frisson went round Old Trafford. By the fifth morning, spectators were being turned away from the gates in their thousands. A remarkable series was about to surpass itself.

THIRD TEST

OLD TRAFFORD 11 – 15 AUGUST 2005

Match drawn

right Michael Vaughan is bowled by a Glenn McGrath no-ball only 45 runs into his magnificent 166. Steve Bucknor extends the arm as Adam Gilchrist, Shane Warne and Ricky Ponting celebrate prematurely.

previous pages
The Old Trafford pavilion is bursting to the rafters with spectators and expectation.

above **Adam Gilchrist tips Michael Vaughan round the corner and a possible wicket becomes four runs.**

left **It's Test victim No. 600 for Shane Warne as Marcus Trescothick makes a hash of a sweep.**

right **All in a day's work ...**

top left **Vaughan unfurls his trademark swivel-pull.**

right Ian Bell, who hit
two fifties in the match,
looks aghast as Brett
Lee appeals for a catch
behind. He looked even
worse when umpire
Bucknor agreed.

opposite, top left
Andrew Flintoff on
the pull. He later
claimed his 46 helped
him feel like a proper
batsman again.

opposite, top right
Simon Katich daren't
look back after
disastrously
shouldering arms
to Flintoff.

opposite, bottom
Ashley Giles is jubilant
after producing the left-
armer's version of the
wonderball to remove
Damien Martyn.

left Shane Warne came within 10 runs
of a maiden Test century by trusting his eye
and chancing his arm.
FRIDAY 5:15 PM

above Adam Gilchrist can't keep up with the
Joneses, Simon and Geraint, who have just
combined to have him caught behind.
FRIDAY 5:42 PM

previous pages **Rarely have Australia been so pleased to see a rainbow on the horizon. The rain which limited Saturday's play to 14 overs probably saved them from defeat.**
SATURDAY 5.52 PM

left **Marcus Trescothick's defensive push against Glenn McGrath did not end up where he intended.**
SUNDAY 1.44 PM

below **Brett Lee prepares to join in the banter with the Old Trafford crowd.**
SUNDAY 4.46 PM

right **Andrew Strauss overcame a blow to the ear to reach his first Ashes century and set up England's declaration.**
SUNDAY 4.53 PM

left Australian fans did
not think much of
Geraint Jones's wicket-
keeping skills.
SUNDAY 5 JULY

above More than 10,000
fans were turned away at
the gates on the final
morning, with a similar
figure told not to leave
Manchester city centre.
MONDAY 6 JULY

previous pages Ricky Ponting's 156 steered Australia to the brink of safety on the final day. But when he was out with 24 balls remaining, his side's hopes hung by a thread.
MONDAY 2.51 PM and 3.32 PM

above Matthew Hoggard and Ian Bell celebrate the wicket of Jason Gillespie – and England have one eye on victory.
MONDAY 4.20 PM

right Shane Warne can hardly believe it as Geraint Jones takes a rebound off Andrew Strauss's knee at second slip.
MONDAY 6.00 PM

left *Ricky Ponting is caught behind down the leg side off Steve Harmison and England have four overs in which to take the final Australian wicket.*

above *Brett Lee punches the air with delight after glancing Harmison's last ball of the match for four. An epic game finishes in a draw.*

above *The crowd's reaction says it all – Australia are delighted with the draw, England downcast.*

THIRD TEST
OLD TRAFFORD

Toss: England
Umpires: BF Bowden (NZ) and SA Bucknor (WI)
Man of the Match: RT Ponting
MATCH DRAWN

ENGLAND 1ST INNINGS

		R	M	B	4	6
ME Trescothick	c Gilchrist b Warne	63	196	117	9	0
AJ Strauss	b Lee	6	43	28	0	0
MP Vaughan*	c McGrath b Katich	166	281	215	20	1
IR Bell	c Gilchrist b Lee	59	205	155	8	0
KP Pietersen	c sub (BJ Hodge) b Lee	21	50	28	1	0
MJ Hoggard	b Lee	4	13	10	1	0
A Flintoff	c Langer b Warne	46	93	67	7	0
GO Jones †	b Gillespie	42	86	51	6	0
AF Giles	c Hayden b Warne	0	11	6	0	0
SJ Harmison	not out	10	13	11	1	0
SP Jones	b Warne	0	7	4	0	0
Extras	(b 4, lb 5, w 3, nb 15)	27				
Total	(113.2 overs, 503 mins)	**444**				

FoW: 1-26 (Strauss, 9.2 ov) 2-163 (Trescothick, 41.5 ov)
3-290 (Vaughan, 74.3 ov) 4-333 (Pietersen, 86.2 ov)
5-341 (Hoggard, 88.6 ov) 6-346 (Bell, 92.1 ov)
7-433 (Flintoff, 109.2 ov) 8-434 (GO Jones, 110.2 ov)
9-438 (Giles, 111.4 ov) 10-444 (SP Jones, 113.2 ov)

BOWLING	O	M	R	W	
McGrath	25	6	86	0	(4nb)
Lee	27	6	100	4	(5nb, 2w)
Gillespie	19	2	114	1	(2nb, 1w)
Warne	33.2	5	99	4	(2nb)
Katich	9	1	36	1	

ENGLAND 2ND INNINGS

		R	M	B	4	6
ME Trescothick	b McGrath	41	71	56	6	0
AJ Strauss	c Martyn b McGrath	106	246	158	9	2
MP Vaughan*	c sub (BJ Hodge) b Lee	14	45	37	2	0
IR Bell	c Katich b McGrath	65	165	103	4	1
KP Pietersen	lbw b McGrath	0	3	1	0	0
A Flintoff	b McGrath	4	20	18	0	0
GO Jones †	not out	27	15	12	2	2
AF Giles	not out	0	4	0	0	0
Extras	(b 5, lb 3, w 1, nb 14)	23				
Total	(61.5 overs, 288 mins)	**280 – 6**				

DNB: MJ Hoggard, SJ Harmison, SP Jones.

FoW: 1-64 (Trescothick, 15.3 ov) 2-97 (Vaughan, 25.4 ov)
3-224 (Strauss, 53.3 ov) 4-225 (Pietersen, 53.5 ov)
5-248 (Flintoff, 59.1 ov) 6-264 (Bell, 61.1 ov)

BOWLING	O	M	R	W	
McGrath	20.5	1	115	5	(6nb, 1w)
Lee	12	0	60	1	(4nb)
Warne	25	3	74	0	
Gillespie	4	0	23	0	(4nb)

AUSTRALIA 1ST INNINGS

		R	M	B	4	6
JL Langer	c Bell b Giles	31	76	50	4	0
ML Hayden	lbw b Giles	34	112	71	5	0
RT Ponting*	c Bell b SP Jones	7	20	12	1	0
DR Martyn	b Giles	20	71	41	2	0
SM Katich	b Flintoff	17	39	28	1	0
AC Gilchrist †	c GO Jones b SP Jones	30	74	49	4	0
SK Warne	c Giles b SP Jones	90	183	122	11	1
MJ Clarke	c Flintoff b SP Jones	7	19	18	0	0
JN Gillespie	lbw b SP Jones	26	144	111	1	1
B Lee	c Trescothick b SP Jones	1	17	16	0	0
GD McGrath	not out	1	20	4	0	0
Extras	(b 8, lb 7, w 8, nb 15)	38				
Total	(84.5 overs, 393 mins)	**302**				

FoW: 1-58 (Langer, 15.5 ov) 2-73 (Ponting, 20.1 ov)
3-86 (Hayden, 23.3 ov) 4-119 (Katich, 32.1 ov)
5-133 (Martyn, 35.3 ov) 6-186 (Gilchrist, 48.1 ov)
7-201 (Clarke, 52.3 ov) 8-287 (Warne, 76.2 ov)
9-293 (Lee, 80.4 ov) 10-302 (Gillespie, 84.5 ov)

BOWLING	O	M	R	W	
Harmison	10	0	47	0	(3nb)
Hoggard	6	2	22	0	
Flintoff	20	1	65	1	(8nb)
SP Jones	17.5	6	53	6	(1nb, 2w)
Giles	31	4	100	3	(1w)

AUSTRALIA 2ND INNINGS (TARGET: 423)

		R	M	B	4	6
JL Langer	c GO Jones b Hoggard	14	42	41	3	0
ML Hayden	b Flintoff	36	123	91	5	1
RT Ponting*	c GO Jones b Harmison	156	411	275	16	1
DR Martyn	lbw b Harmison	19	53	36	3	0
SM Katich	c Giles b Flintoff	12	30	23	2	0
AC Gilchrist †	c Bell b Flintoff	4	36	30	0	0
MJ Clarke	b SP Jones	39	73	63	7	0
JN Gillespie	lbw b Hoggard	0	8	5	0	0
SK Warne	c GO Jones b Flintoff	34	99	69	5	0
B Lee	not out	18	44	25	4	0
GD McGrath	not out	5	17	9	1	0
Extras	(b 5, lb 8, w 1, nb 20)	34				
Total	(108 overs, 474 mins)	**371 – 9**				

FoW: 1-25 (Langer, 11.1 ov) 2-96 (Hayden, 29.4 ov)
3-129 (Martyn, 42.5 ov) 4-165 (Katich, 49.3 ov)
5-182 (Gilchrist, 57.4 ov) 6-263 (Clarke, 75.2 ov)
7-264 (Gillespie, 76.5 ov) 8-340 (Warne, 98.2 ov)
9-354 (Ponting, 103.6 ov)

BOWLING	O	M	R	W	
Harmison	22	4	67	2	(4nb, 1w)
Hoggard	13	0	49	2	(6nb)
Giles	26	4	93	0	
Vaughan	5	0	21	0	
Flintoff	25	6	71	4	(9nb)
SP Jones	17	3	57	1	

The odds favoured Australia, who needed to win only one of the last two Tests to retain the Ashes. But the momentum was with England, despite their failure to take the final wicket at Old Trafford. Australia spent the time between the third and fourth Tests trying to work out a method of combating the reverse-swing England had been using so effectively. "It's like trying to solve a puzzle," admitted Justin Langer. But there were more pressing problems, and Australia's task became harder when Glenn McGrath dropped out at the last minute with an injury to his right elbow. To no one's great surprise, England named the same XI that had come so close at Manchester. After two nail-biters, the nation's collective blood pressure needed a tame draw or a one-sided win. It got neither.

FOURTH TEST

TRENT BRIDGE 25 - 28 AUGUST 2005

England won by three wickets

above Glenn McGrath's injury
and Jason Gillespie's poor form
meant a Test debut for the
22-year-old Shaun Tait. He
responded with three wickets.
THURSDAY 11.52 am

right Marcus Trescothick's solid
series continued with a meaty 65.
THURSDAY 11.52 am

previous pages The mobile
generation: Kevin Pietersen,
Steve Harmison and Michael
Vaughan spread the word about
England's victory.
SUNDAY 7.34 pm

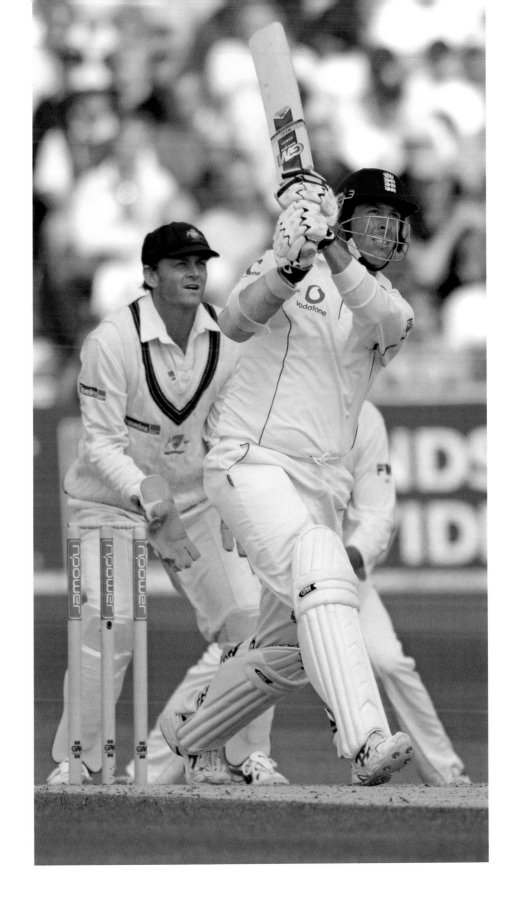

left Shaun Tait fires an 86mph yorker through Marcus Trescothick's defences to open his Test account.
THURSDAY 3:56 PM

above His second wicket did not take long: four overs later Ian Bell nibbles, Adam Gilchrist clings on, and England are 146 for three.
THURSDAY 4:11 PM

opposite At Edgbaston it was his ankle; at Trent Bridge his elbow. Glenn McGrath would not have expected to carry the drinks.

left After missing the previous three Ashes series, Andrew Flintoff makes up for lost time with his first century against Australia. Trent Bridge goes wild.

below Flintoff's partner-in-crime Geraint Jones is 15 runs away from a maiden Ashes hundred of his own when he is caught and bowled by Michael Kasprowicz.

The clouds are gathering over Australia's hopes as Simon Jones traps Ricky Ponting leg-before.

Ian Bell has just caught Justin Langer at short leg off Matthew Hoggard. Langer knows it, and Australia are in trouble at 58 for four.

For the second time in the series, Steve Harmison removes Michael Clarke in the last over the day. England are cock-a-hoop.

previous pages **The catch of the series: Andrew Strauss defies gravity to get rid of Adam Gilchrist, and Australia are about to follow on for the first time since 1988-89.**

SATURDAY 11.27 am

left **The sequence in full.**

SATURDAY 11.27 am

above **Ricky Ponting is run out by a direct hit from cover by Gary Pratt, England's substitute fielder. Ponting's subsequent volley of abuse at the England dressing-room cost him 75% of his match fee.**

SATURDAY 4.29 pm

above Geraint Jones's keeping always felt as if it was
one fumble away from disaster. Here, he misses a
stumping chance with Michael Clarke stranded.

right Simon Katich cannot hide his anger after
receiving a poor lbw decision against Steve Harmison.
His outburst put paid to half his match fee.

above **Michael Vaughan is caught at slip off Shane Warne and England's pursuit of 129 is tottering at 31 for two.**
SUNDAY 4:15 PM

left **Andrew Strauss nudges Warne to leg slip and it's 57 for three.**
SUNDAY 4:28 PM

top right **Brett Lee bowls an incredulous Andrew Flintoff: 111 for six.**
SUNDAY 5:53 PM

right **Warne celebrates the wicket of Geraint Jones: 116 for seven.**
SUNDAY 6:07 PM

left **Ashley Giles pricks the tension by working Shane Warne through midwicket for the winning runs.**

above **Andrew Flintoff looks set to explode as the England balcony celebrates.**

right **Giles and Matthew Hoggard: two unlikely batting heroes.**

above **Tired and emotional:
Andrew Flintoff winds
down with a quick chat, a
bottle of beer, and the
team mascot.**
SUNDAY 7.35 PM

FOURTH TEST

TRENT BRIDGE

Toss: England

Umpires: Aleem Dar (Pak) and SA Bucknor (WI)

Man of the Match: A Flintoff

ENGLAND WON BY THREE WICKETS

ENGLAND 1ST INNINGS		R	M	B	4	6
ME Trescothick	b Tait	65	138	111	8	1
AJ Strauss	c Hayden b Warne	35	99	64	4	0
MP Vaughan*	c Gilchrist b Ponting	58	138	99	9	0
IR Bell	c Gilchrist b Tait	3	12	5	0	0
KP Pietersen	c Gilchrist b Lee	45	131	108	6	0
A Flintoff	lbw b Tait	102	201	132	14	1
GO Jones †	c & b Kasprowicz	85	205	149	8	0
AF Giles	lbw b Warne	15	45	35	3	0
MJ Hoggard	c Gilchrist b Warne	10	46	28	1	0
SJ Harmison	st Gilchrist b Warne	2	9	6	0	0
SP Jones	not out	15	32	27	3	0
Extras	(b 1, lb 15, w 1, nb 25)	42				
Total	(123.1 overs, 537 mins)	**477**				

FoW: 1-105 (Strauss, 21.4 ov) 2-137 (Trescothick, 30.5 ov)
3-146 (Bell, 34.1 ov) 4-213 (Vaughan, 55.2 ov)
5-241 (Pietersen, 64.1 ov) 6-418 (Flintoff, 103.2 ov)
7-450 (GO Jones, 112.5 ov) 8-450 (Giles, 113.1 ov)
9-454 (Harmison, 115.1 ov) 10-477 (Hoggard, 123.1 ov)

BOWLING	O	M	R	W	
Lee	32	2	131	1	(8nb)
Kasprowicz	32	3	122	1	(13nb)
Tait	24	4	97	3	(4nb)
Warne	29.1	4	102	4	
Ponting	6	2	9	1	(1w)

AUSTRALIA 1ST INNINGS		R	M	B	4	6
JL Langer	c Bell b Hoggard	27	95	59	5	0
ML Hayden	lbw b Hoggard	7	41	27	1	0
RT Ponting*	lbw b SP Jones	1	6	6	0	0
DR Martyn	lbw b Hoggard	1	4	3	0	0
MJ Clarke	lbw b Harmison	36	93	53	5	0
SM Katich	c Strauss b SP Jones	45	91	66	7	0
AC Gilchrist †	c Strauss b Flintoff	27	58	36	3	1
SK Warne	c Bell b SP Jones	0	2	1	0	0
B Lee	c Bell b SP Jones	47	51	44	5	3
MS Kasprowicz	b SP Jones	5	8	7	1	0
SW Tait	not out	3	27	9	0	0
Extras	(lb 2, w 1, nb 16)	19				
Total	(49.1 overs, 247 mins)	**218**				

FoW: 1-20 (Hayden, 9.3 ov) 2-21 (Ponting, 10.3 ov)
3-22 (Martyn, 11.1 ov) 4-58 (Langer, 19.3 ov),
5-99 (Clarke, 30.3 ov) 6-157 (Katich, 39.2 ov),
7-157 (Warne, 39.3 ov) 8-163 (Gilchrist, 42.2 ov),
9-175 (Kasprowicz, 43.2 ov) 10-218 (Lee, 49.1 ov).

BOWLING	O	M	R	W	
Harmison	9	1	48	1	(3nb)
Hoggard	15	3	70	3	(4nb)
SP Jones	14.1	4	44	5	(1nb)
Flintoff	11	1	54	1	(8nb, 1w)

AUSTRALIA 2ND INNINGS (FOLLOWING ON)		R	M	B	4	6
JL Langer	c Bell b Giles	61	149	112	8	0
ML Hayden	c Giles b Flintoff	26	57	41	4	0
RT Ponting*	run out (sub [GJ Pratt])	48	137	89	3	1
DR Martyn	c GO Jones b Flintoff	13	56	30	1	0
MJ Clarke	c GO Jones b Hoggard	56	209	170	6	0
SM Katich	lbw b Harmison	59	262	183	4	0
AC Gilchrist †	lbw b Hoggard	11	20	11	2	0
SK Warne	st GO Jones b Giles	45	68	42	5	2
B Lee	not out	26	77	39	3	0
MS Kasprowicz	c GO Jones b Harmison	19	30	26	1	0
SW Tait	b Harmison	4	20	16	1	0
Extras	(b 1, lb 4, nb 14)	19				
Total	(124 overs, 548 mins)	**387**				

FoW: 1-50 (Hayden, 13.4 ov) 2-129 (Langer, 33.6 ov)
3-155 (Ponting, 44.1 ov) 4-161 (Martyn, 46.1 ov)
5-261 (Clarke, 94.2 ov) 6-277 (Gilchrist, 98.5 ov)
7-314 (Katich, 107.3 ov) 8-342 (Warne, 112.3 ov)
9-373 (Kasprowicz, 119.2 ov) 10-387 (Tait, 123.6 ov)

BOWLING	O	M	R	W	
Hoggard	27	7	72	2	(1nb)
SP Jones	4	0	15	0	
Harmison	30	5	93	3	(1nb)
Flintoff	29	4	83	2	(9nb)
Giles	28	3	107	2	
Bell	6	2	12	0	(3nb)

ENGLAND 2ND INNINGS (TARGET: 129)		R	M	B	4	6
ME Trescothick	c Ponting b Warne	27	24	22	4	0
AJ Strauss	c Clarke b Warne	23	68	37	3	0
MP Vaughan*	c Hayden b Warne	0	8	6	0	0
IR Bell	c Kasprowicz b Lee	3	38	20	0	0
KP Pietersen	c Gilchrist b Lee	23	51	34	3	0
A Flintoff	b Lee	26	63	34	3	0
GO Jones †	c Kasprowicz b Warne	3	25	13	0	0
AF Giles	not out	7	30	17	0	0
MJ Hoggard	not out	8	20	13	1	0
Extras	(lb 4, nb 5)	9				
Total	(31.5 overs, 168 mins)	**129 – 7**				

DNB: SJ Harmison, SP Jones.

FoW: 1-32 (Trescothick, 5.1 ov) 2-36 (Vaughan, 7.1 ov)
3-57 (Strauss, 13.5 ov) 4-57 (Bell, 14.1 ov)
5-103 (Pietersen, 24.1 ov) 6-111 (Flintoff, 26.4 ov)
7-116 (GO Jones, 27.6 ov)

BOWLING	O	M	R	W	
Lee	12	0	51	3	(5nb)
Kasprowicz	2	0	19	0	
Warne	13.5	2	31	4	
Tait	4	0	24	0	

Ashes fever had by now overwhelmed the country, and only those who had recently returned from a holiday on Mars were unaware of the facts: England needed to avoid defeat to reclaim a prize they had lost 16 years earlier. Michael Vaughan admitted his side were "on the verge of something special". Ricky Ponting said: "If the guys can't lift themselves, they shouldn't be playing." There was simply too much at stake to think too far ahead, and one British tabloid captured the mood of nervous tension with a front-page prayer for rain. The pre-Test psychology swung Australia's way when Simon Jones pulled out with an ankle injury and Glenn McGrath was pronounced fit. But then England won the toss on a sunny Thursday morning. The moment of truth had arrived.

FIFTH TEST

THE OVAL 8 – 12 SEPTEMBER 2005

Match drawn

above Mark Nicholas and Ranjan Madugalle oversee the toss as Michael Vaughan and Ricky Ponting wait anxiously. Ponting calls incorrectly, and England bat first.
THURSDAY 10.02 AM

previous pages It's **3.10pm** and the Australians reckon the light is good enough for some cricket. Their sunglasses are a light-hearted dig at the umpires.
SUNDAY 3.10 PM

top right Matthew Hayden snaps up Marcus Trescothick to give Shane Warne the first of his 12 wickets in the match.
THURSDAY 11.48 AM

right Kevin Pietersen plays round a leg-break and England are suddenly **131 for four.** Warne has the lot.
THURSDAY 1.36 PM

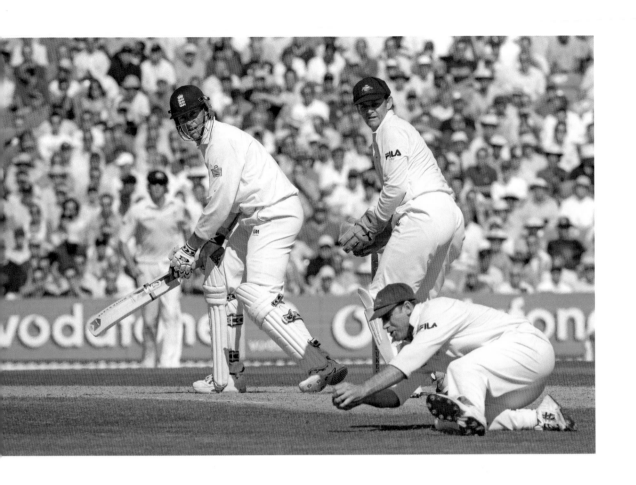

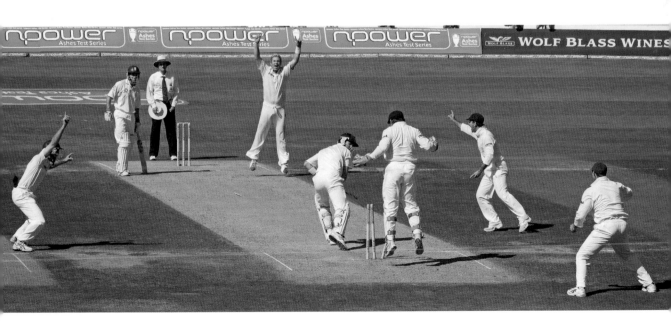

The first day was all
about two men. Andrew
Strauss *left* hit 129 to
ensure against an
England collapse ...

... and Shane Warne
above and below took
five wickets as England
closed on 319 for seven.

above **Justin Langer immediately takes the long handle to Ashley Giles ...**

top right **... with spectator-scattering consequences.**

right **Others watched from equally precarious vantage points.**

above Durham's Gary Pratt became a minor
celebrity after running out Ricky Ponting at
Trent Bridge. At The Oval he was cheered
every time he touched the ball.
FRIDAY 2.47 PM

right Justin Langer's off-bail tells the story
as Steve Harmison strikes, but not before
Australia's openers have added 185.
Langer's share is 105.
SATURDAY 1.56 PM

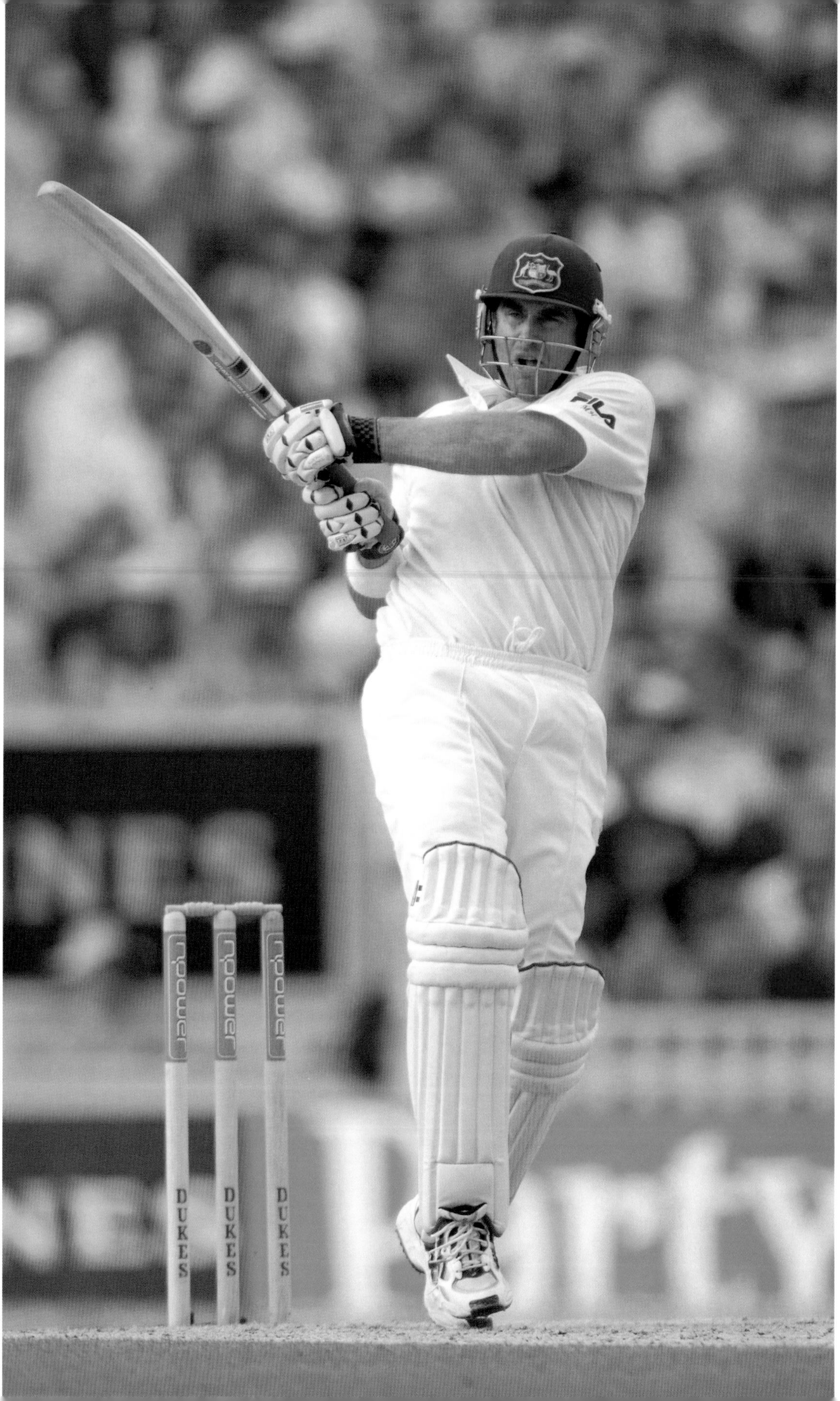
FILA
DUKES
DUKES
DUKES

left **Matthew Hayden's miserable sequence – he failed to reach 40 in the first four Tests – ended at The Oval with a patient 138.**
SATURDAY 4 02 PM

above **Steve Harmison adds his congratulations.**
SATURDAY 4.26 PM

right **England prayed for rain and on Saturday it arrived. The umbrellas went up with relish.**
SATURDAY 4.30 PM

top left Michael Clarke
becomes the second of
four quick victims for
Matthew Hoggard as
Australia stutter.

left Ashley Giles catches
Brett Lee at cow corner
and Australia have lost
their last seven wickets
for 44 runs.

above Australia's
response is immediate as
Shane Warne removes
Andrew Strauss for two.
The stage is set for
another nerve-jangler.

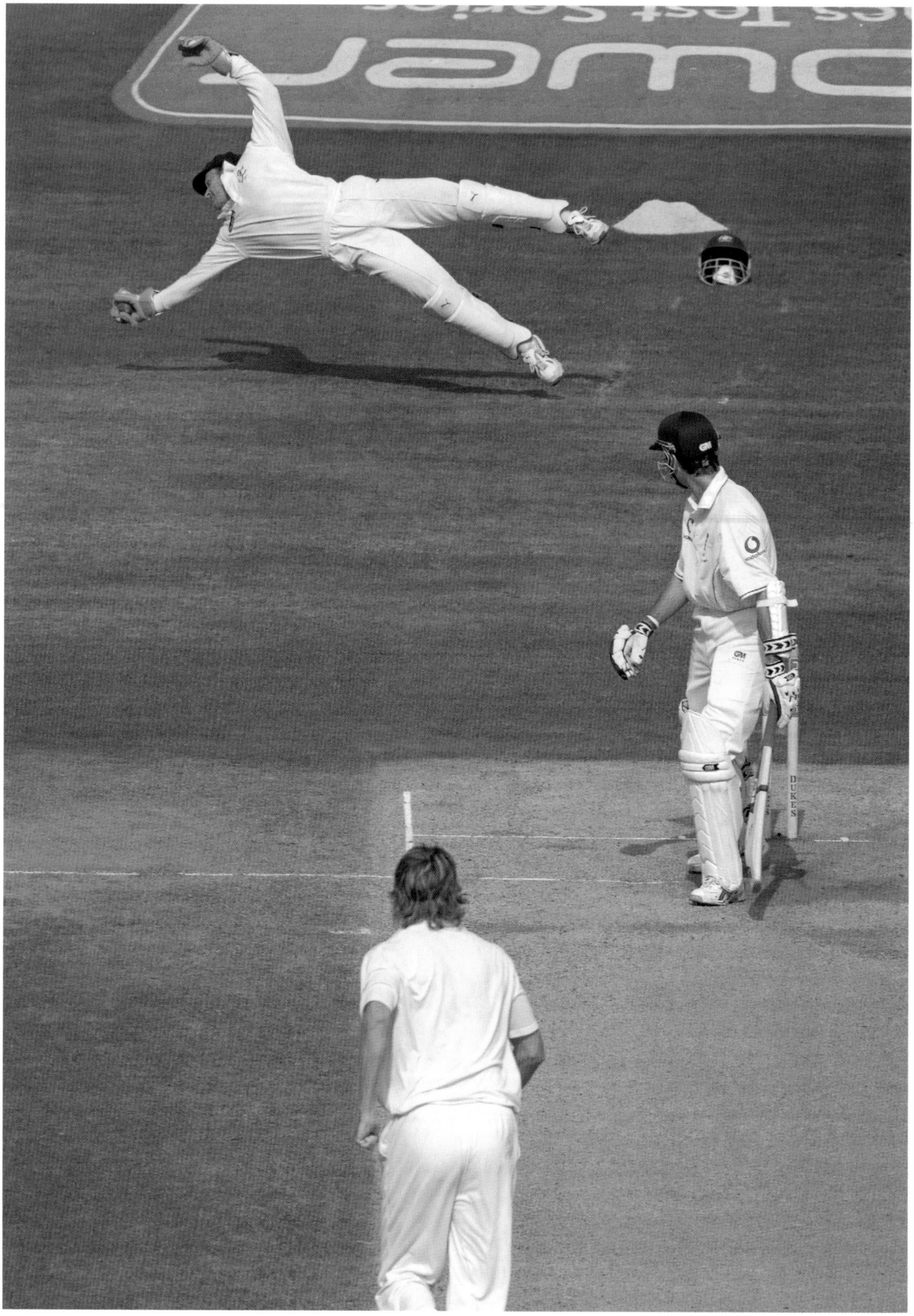
DUKES

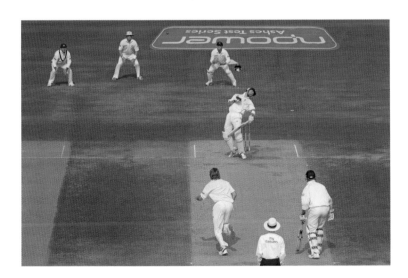

opposite *Adam Gilchrist swoops to dismiss Michael Vaughan off Glenn McGrath and England are 67 for two.*

above *Next ball, Ian Bell edges to slip and Australia scent blood.*

left *The hat-trick ball is a whisker away from claiming Kevin Pietersen, but the ball balloons to second slip off his shoulder rather than his bat. England breathe again.*

left **Was this the moment that cost Australia the Ashes?**
Kevin Pietersen, on 15, edges Brett Lee but for once Shane
Warne cannot hold on.

above **His bowling, though, was in a different class, and the wicket**
of Andrew Flintoff, caught and bowled, left England 126 for five
just before lunch. The fate of the Ashes is in the balance ...

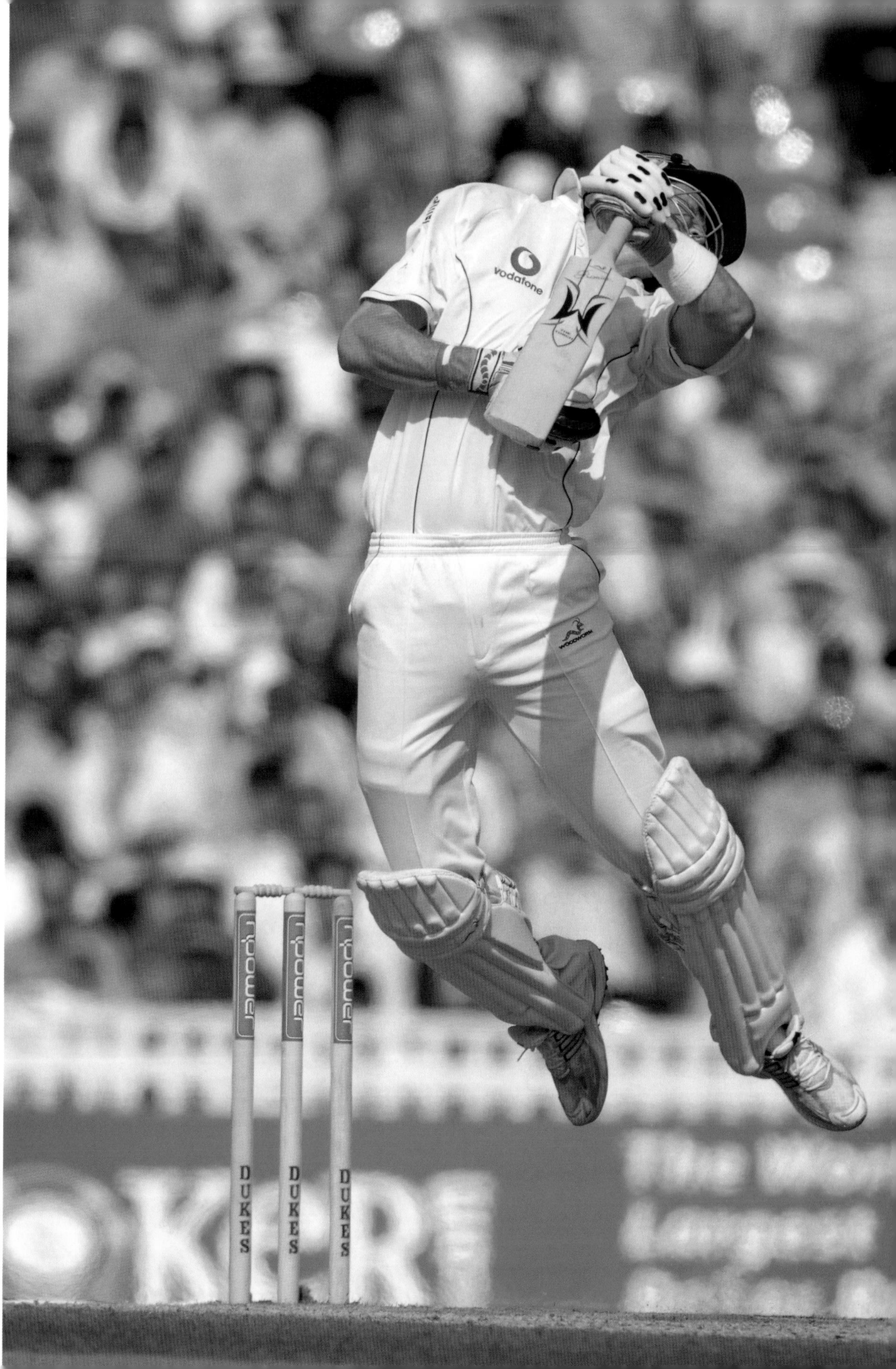
vodafone
DUKES
DUKES
DUKES

left **Kevin Pietersen
survives a ferocious Brett
Lee over just before lunch.
It made him determined
to go out after the break
and play his shots.**
MONDAY 12.32 PM

right **Pietersen hammers
a pull down the ground
off Lee and the
counter-attack is on.**
MONDAY 1.43 PM

below and below right
**Pietersen's seven sixes
were the most by an
England player in an
Ashes innings – not to
mention by a cricketer
with a dead-skunk haircut.**
MONDAY 4.43 PM

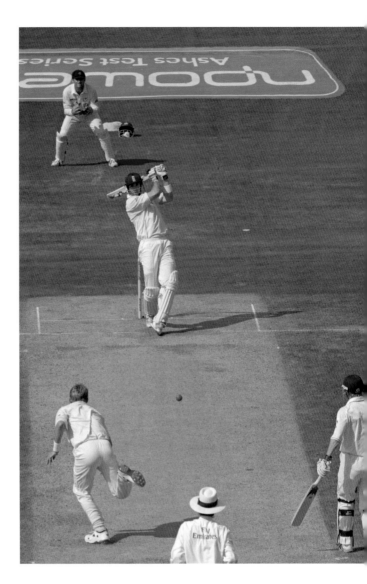

above Kevin Pietersen's 158 stole the headlines, but Ashley Giles's 59 was almost as important. His stand of 109 for the eighth wicket with Pietersen was the final nail in Australia's coffin.

top right The end of an era as Glenn McGrath and Shane Warne leave an English Test ground together probably for the last time. Their combined wicket haul is 1,141.

bottom right Justin Langer discusses the light with Billy Bowden and Rudi Koertzen, and the game is almost over. Moments later, it is abandoned and England's celebrations begin.

FIFTH TEST

THE OVAL

Toss: England
Umpires: BF Bowden (NZ) and RE Koertzen (SA)
Man of the Match: KP Pietersen

ENGLAND 1ST INNINGS		R	M	B	4	6
ME Trescothick	c Hayden b Warne	43	77	65	8	0
AJ Strauss	c Katich b Warne	129	351	210	17	0
MP Vaughan*	c Clarke b Warne	11	26	25	2	0
IR Bell	lbw b Warne	0	9	7	0	0
KP Pietersen	b Warne	14	30	25	2	0
A Flintoff	c Warne b McGrath	72	162	115	12	1
PD Collingwood	lbw b Tait	7	26	26	1	0
GO Jones †	b Lee	25	60	41	5	0
AF Giles	lbw b Warne	32	120	70	1	0
MJ Hoggard	c Martyn b McGrath	2	47	36	0	0
SJ Harmison	not out	20	25	20	4	0
Extras	(b 4, lb 6, w 1, nb 7)	18				
Total	**(105.3 overs, 471 mins)**	**373**				

FoW: 1-82 (Trescothick, 17.3 ov) 2-102 (Vaughan, 23.5 ov)
3-104 (Bell, 25.6 ov) 4-131 (Pietersen, 33.3 ov)
5-274 (Flintoff, 70.1 ov) 6-289 (Collingwood, 76.3 ov)
7-297 (Strauss, 79.4 ov) 8-325 (Jones, 89.3 ov)
9-345 (Hoggard, 100.2 ov) 10-373 (Giles, 105.3 ov)

BOWLING	O	M	R	W	
McGrath	27	5	72	2	(1w)
Lee	23	3	94	1	(3nb)
Tait	15	1	61	1	(3nb)
Warne	37.3	5	122	6	
Katich	3	0	14	0	

ENGLAND 2ND INNINGS		R	M	B	4	6
ME Trescothick	lbw b Warne	33	150	84	1	0
AJ Strauss	c Katich b Warne	1	16	7	0	0
MP Vaughan*	c Gilchrist b McGrath	45	80	65	6	0
IR Bell	c Warne b McGrath	0	2	1	0	0
KP Pietersen	b McGrath	158	285	187	15	7
A Flintoff	c & b Warne	8	20	13	1	0
PD Collingwood	c Ponting b Warne	10	72	51	1	0
GO Jones †	b Tait	1	24	12	0	0
AF Giles	b Warne	59	159	97	7	0
MJ Hoggard	not out	4	45	35	0	0
SJ Harmison	c Hayden b Warne	0	2	2	0	0
Extras	(b 4, w 7, nb 5)	16				
Total	**(91.3 overs, 432 mins)**	**335**				

FoW: 1-2 (Strauss, 3.4 ov) 2-67 (Vaughan, 22.4 ov)
3-67 (Bell, 22.5 ov) 4-109 (Trescothick, 33.1 ov)
5-126 (Flintoff, 37.5 ov) 6-186 (Collingwood, 51.5 ov)
7-199 (Jones, 56.5 ov) 8-308 (Pietersen, 82.5 ov)
9-335 (Giles, 91.1 ov) 10-335 (Harmison, 91.3 ov)

BOWLING	O	M	R	W	
McGrath	26	3	85	3	(1nb)
Lee	20	4	88	0	(4nb, 1w)
Warne	38.3	3	124	6	(1w)
Clarke	2	0	6	0	
Tait	5	0	28	1	(1w)

AUSTRALIA 1ST INNINGS		R	M	B	4	6
JL Langer	b Harmison	105	233	146	11	2
ML Hayden	lbw b Flintoff	138	416	303	18	0
RT Ponting*	c Strauss b Flintoff	35	81	56	3	0
DR Martyn	c Collingwood b Flintoff	10	36	29	1	0
MJ Clarke	lbw b Hoggard	25	119	59	2	0
SM Katich	lbw b Flintoff	1	12	11	0	0
AC Gilchrist †	lbw b Hoggard	23	32	20	4	0
SK Warne	c Vaughan b Flintoff	0	18	10	0	0
B Lee	c Giles b Hoggard	6	22	10	0	0
GD McGrath	c Strauss b Hoggard	0	6	6	0	0
SW Tait	not out	1	7	2	0	0
Extras	(b 4, lb 8, w 2, nb 9)	23				
Total	**(107.1 overs, 494 mins)**	**367**				

FoW: 1-185 (Langer, 52.4 ov) 2-264 (Ponting, 72.2 ov)
3-281 (Martyn, 80.4 ov) 4-323 (Hayden, 92.3 ov)
5-329 (Katich, 94.6 ov) 6-356 (Gilchrist, 101.1 ov)
7-359 (Clarke, 103.3 ov) 8-363 (Warne, 104.5 ov)
9-363 (McGrath, 105.6 ov) 10-367 (Lee, 107.1 ov)

BOWLING	O	M	R	W	
Harmison	22	2	87	1	(2nb, 2w)
Hoggard	24.1	2	97	4	(1nb)
Flintoff	34	10	78	5	(6nb)
Giles	23	1	76	0	
Collingwood	4	0	17	0	

AUSTRALIA 2ND INNINGS (TARGET: 342)		R	M	B	4	6
JL Langer	not out	0	3	4	0	0
ML Hayden	not out	0	3	0	0	0
Extras	(lb 4)	4				
Total	**(0.4 overs, 3 mins)**	**4 – 0**				

DNB: RT Ponting*, DR Martyn, MJ Clarke, SM Katich,
AC Gilchrist †, SK Warne, B Lee, GD McGrath, SW Tait.

BOWLING	O	M	R	W
Harmison	0.4	0	0	0

ENGLAND WON THE SERIES 2-1

England's Man of the Series: A Flintoff

Australia's Man of the Series: SK Warne

The Compton-Miller Medal: A Flintoff

"It's been the best series I've ever been part of.
England thoroughly deserve to regain the Ashes."

Ricky Ponting

"Cricket has captured the nation. You have a dream
when you are growing up, but this is more than a dream."

Michael Vaughan

SERIES AVERAGES

AUSTRALIA BATTING AND FIELDING

Name	M	I	NO	Runs	HS	Ave	SR	100	50	Ct	St
JL Langer	5	10	1	394	105	43.77	58.63	1	2	2	-
RT Ponting	5	9	0	359	156	39.88	59.63	1	1	4	-
MJ Clarke	5	9	0	335	91	37.22	54.38	-	2	2	-
GD McGrath	3	5	4	36	20*	36.00	63.15	-	-	1	-
ML Hayden	5	10	1	318	138	35.33	46.97	1	-	10	-
SK Warne	5	9	0	249	90	27.66	70.53	-	1	5	-
SM Katich	5	9	0	248	67	27.55	46.79	-	2	4	-
B Lee	5	9	3	158	47	26.33	65.02	-	-	2	-
AC Gilchrist	5	9	1	181	49*	22.62	71.82	-	-	18	1
DR Martyn	5	9	0	178	65	19.77	53.13	-	1	4	-
MS Kasprowicz	2	4	0	44	20	11.00	67.69	-	-	3	-
SW Tait	2	3	2	8	4	8.00	29.62	-	-	-	-
JN Gillespie	3	6	0	47	26	7.83	21.55	-	-	1	-

AUSTRALIA BOWLING

Name	M	O	M	R	W	Ave	Best	5w	10m	SR	Econ
SK Warne	5	252.5	37	797	40	19.92	6-46	3	2	37.9	3.15
GD McGrath	3	134	22	440	19	23.15	5-53	2	-	42.3	3.28
B Lee	5	191.1	25	822	20	41.10	4-82	-	-	57.3	4.29
SW Tait	2	48	5	210	5	42.00	3-97	-	-	57.6	4.37
MS Kasprowicz	2	52	6	250	4	62.50	3-80	-	-	78.0	4.80
JN Gillespie	3	67	6	300	3	100.00	2-91	-	-	134.0	4.47

Also bowled: RT Ponting 6-2-9-1, SM Katich 12-1-50-1, MJ Clarke 2-0-6-0.

ENGLAND BATTING AND FIELDING

Name	M	I	NO	Runs	HS	Ave	SR	100	50	Ct	St
KP Pietersen	5	10	1	473	158	52.55	71.45	1	3	-	-
ME Trescothick	5	10	0	431	90	43.10	60.27	-	3	3	-
A Flintoff	5	10	0	402	102	40.20	74.16	1	3	3	-
AJ Strauss	5	10	0	393	129	39.30	57.79	2	-	6	-
SP Jones	4	6	4	66	20*	33.00	67.34	-	-	1	-
MP Vaughan	5	10	0	326	166	32.60	60.82	1	1	2	-
GO Jones	5	10	1	229	85	25.44	57.97	-	1	15	1
AF Giles	5	10	2	155	59	19.37	50.65	-	1	5	-
IR Bell	5	10	0	171	65	17.10	45.35	-	2	8	-
SJ Harmison	5	8	2	60	20*	10.00	84.50	-	-	1	-
MJ Hoggard	5	9	2	45	16	6.42	19.65	-	-	-	-

Also batted: PD Collingwood (one match) 10, 7.

ENGLAND BOWLING

Name	M	O	M	R	W	Ave	Best	5w	10m	SR	Econ
SP Jones	4	102	17	378	18	21.00	6-53	2	-	34.0	3.70
A Flintoff	5	194	32	655	24	27.29	5-78	1	-	48.5	3.37
MJ Hoggard	5	122.1	15	473	16	29.56	4-97	-	-	45.8	3.87
SJ Harmison	5	161.1	22	549	17	32.29	5-43	1	-	56.8	3.40
AF Giles	5	160	18	578	10	57.80	3-78	-	-	96.0	3.61

Also bowled: PD Collingwood 4-0-17-0, IR Bell 7-2-20-0, MP Vaughan 5-0-21-0.

Key: In the batting and fielding tables, SR is the batsman's strike-rate, or number of runs scored per 100 balls faced.
In the bowling tables, it quantifies the number of balls per wicket.